Contents

Healthy teeth

When I smile, you can see my **teeth**.
Mum says I have a nice smile.

She gives me crunchy carrots and juicy apples to eat.

They help to keep my teeth strong and healthy.

I **clean** my teeth when I wake up.

I clean them again when I go to bed.

6

Today, I'm going to show the **dentist** my teeth.

It is my first visit to the dentist.

The waiting room

The dentist is busy looking at someone else's teeth.

Mum and I look at a book in the waiting room.

It's my turn!

The dental nurse calls my name. She says Mum can come, too.

The dentist's chair

I see a big blue chair that is like a bed.

There is also a little basin and a cup of pink water.

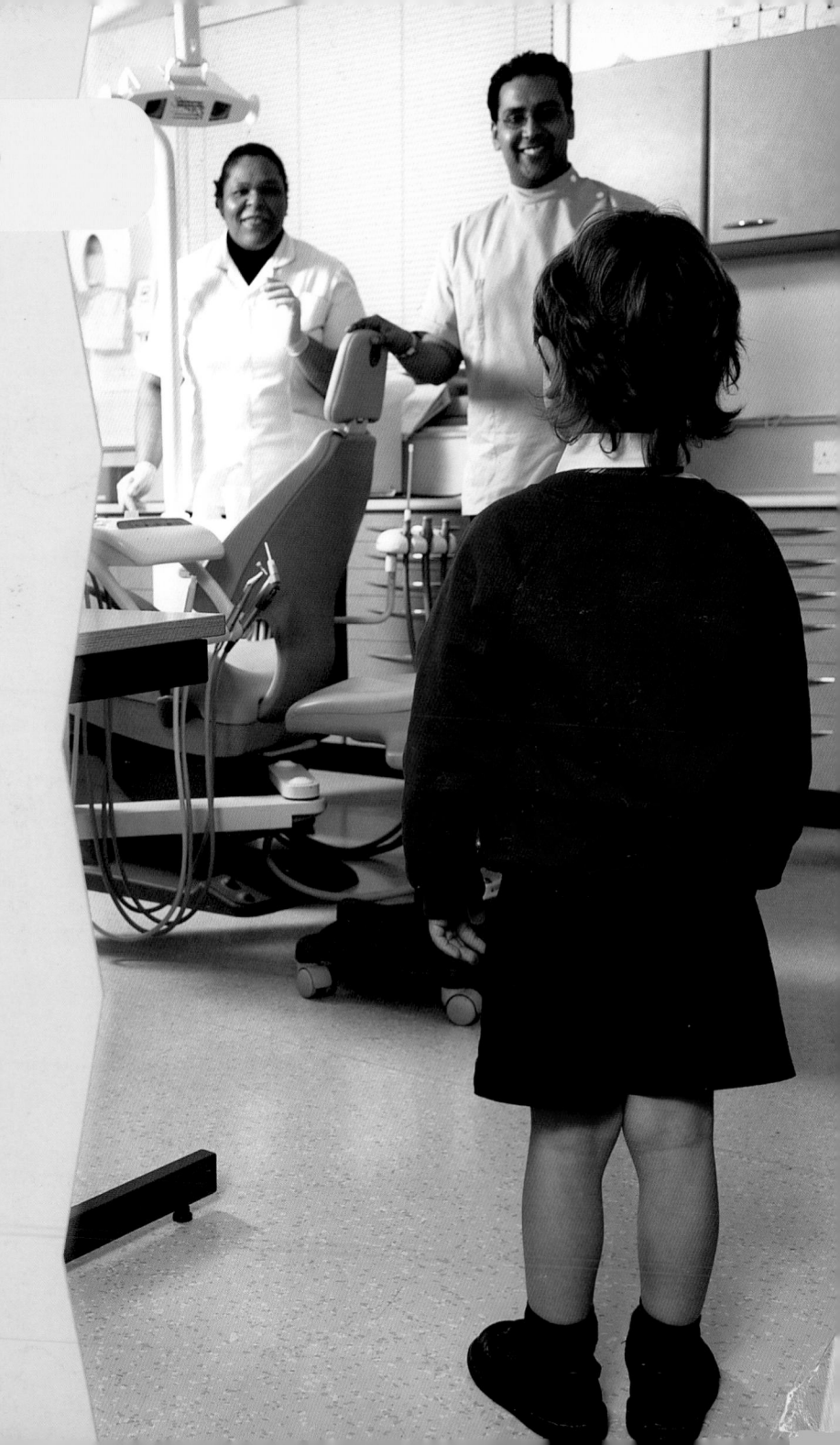

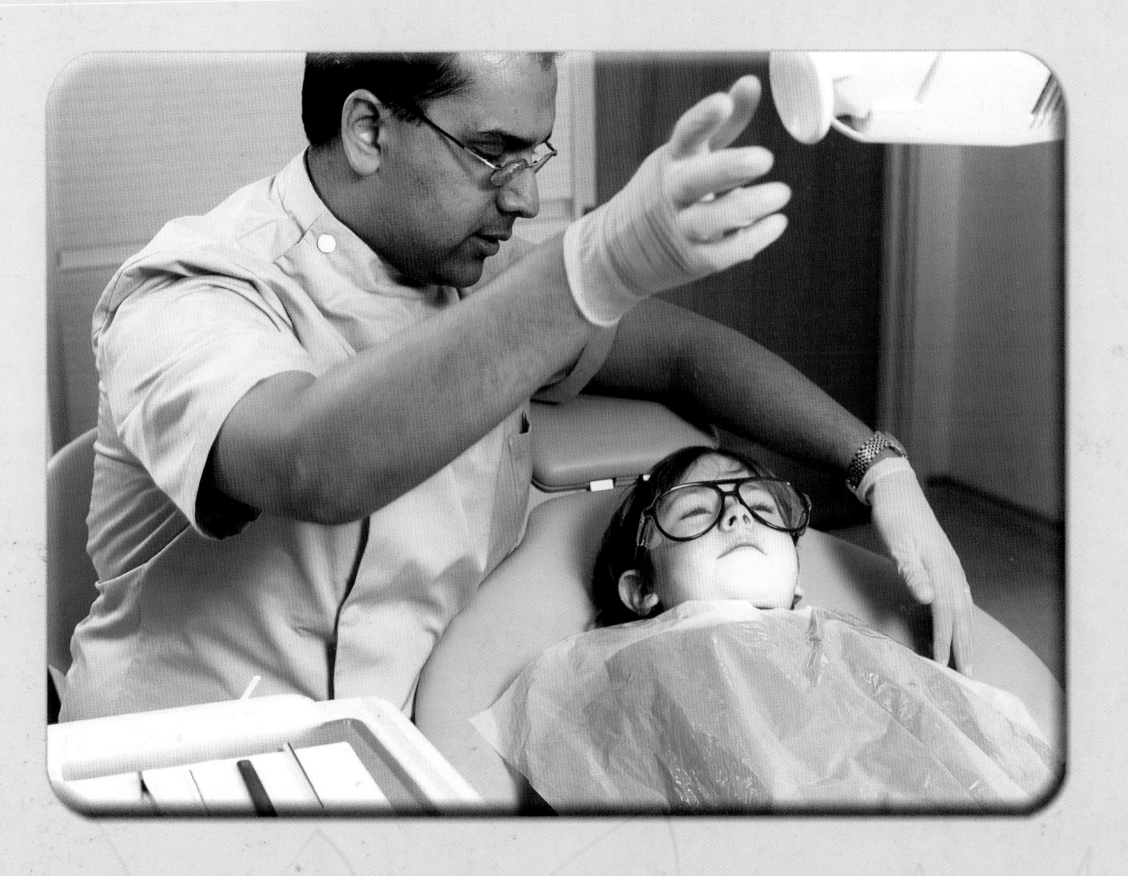

"Come and sit in the magic chair,"
says the dentist.

The chair goes up and down.

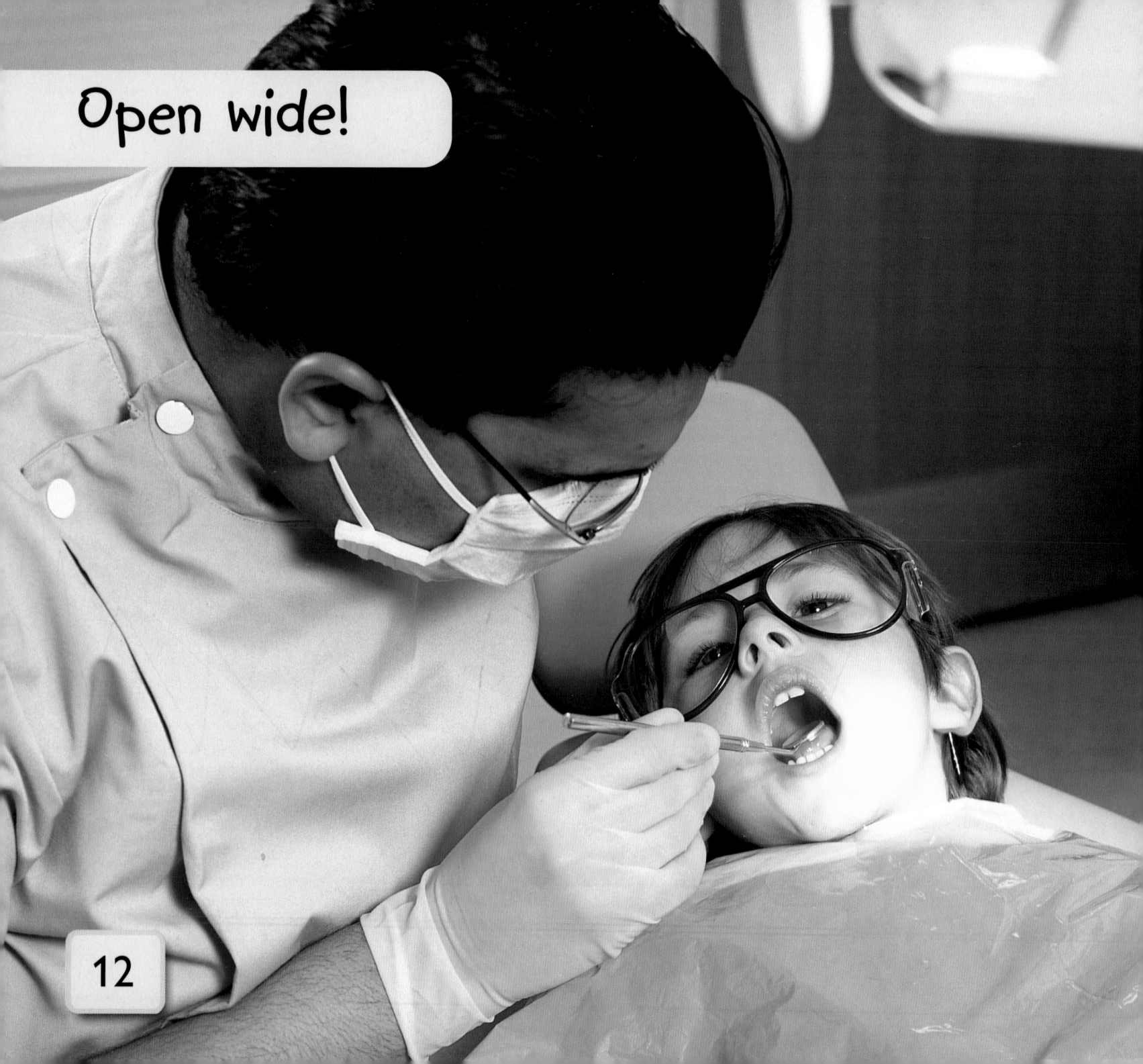

Open wide!

"Open wide," says the dentist.
I open my **mouth** very wide!

The light shines into my mouth.

The dentist uses a little mirror
to look at all my teeth.

How many teeth?

The dentist counts my teeth.

Ten on the top and ten
on the bottom.
I have twenty teeth!

Then he puffs my teeth
dry with a puffer.

It feels a bit cold.

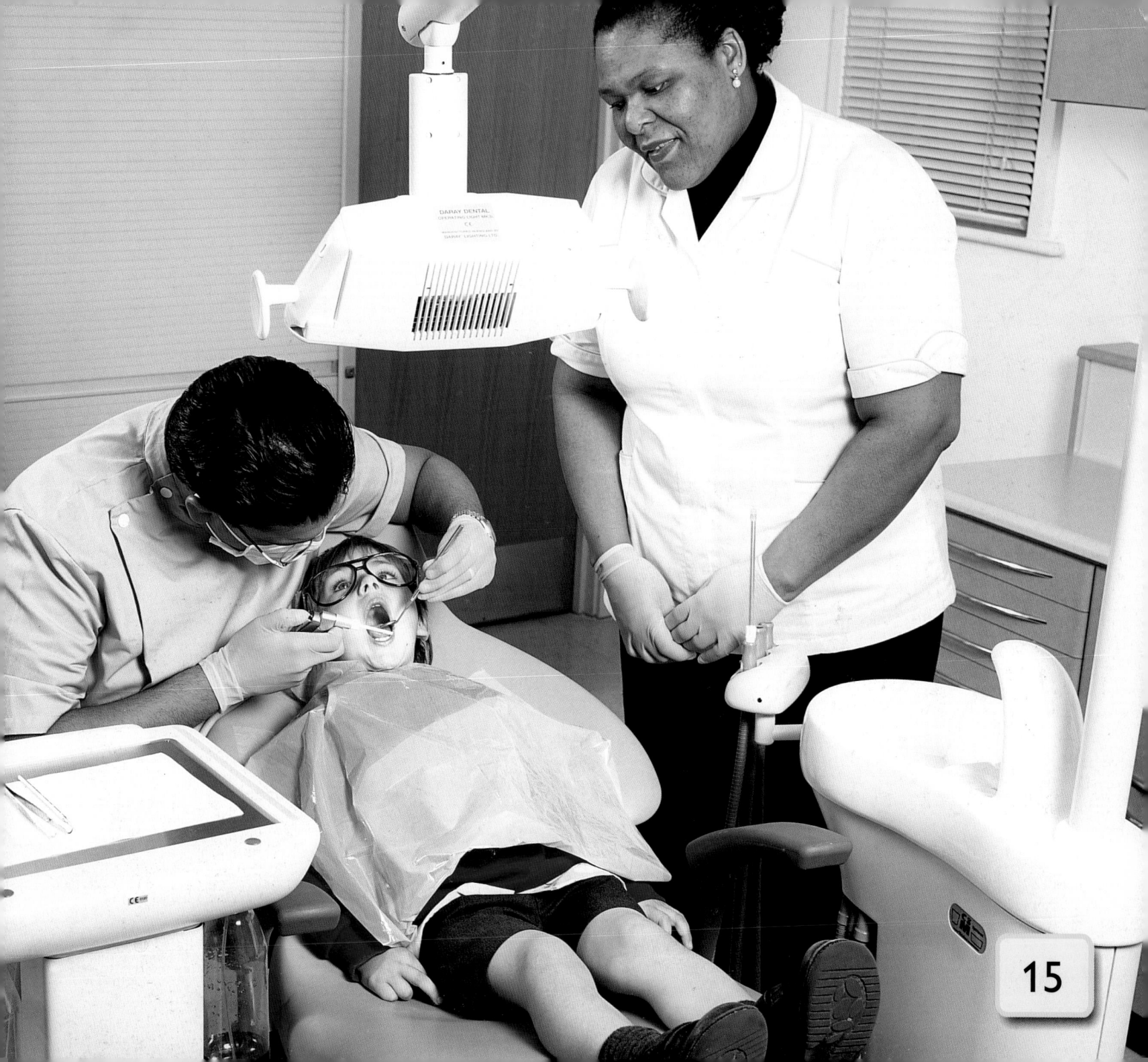

15

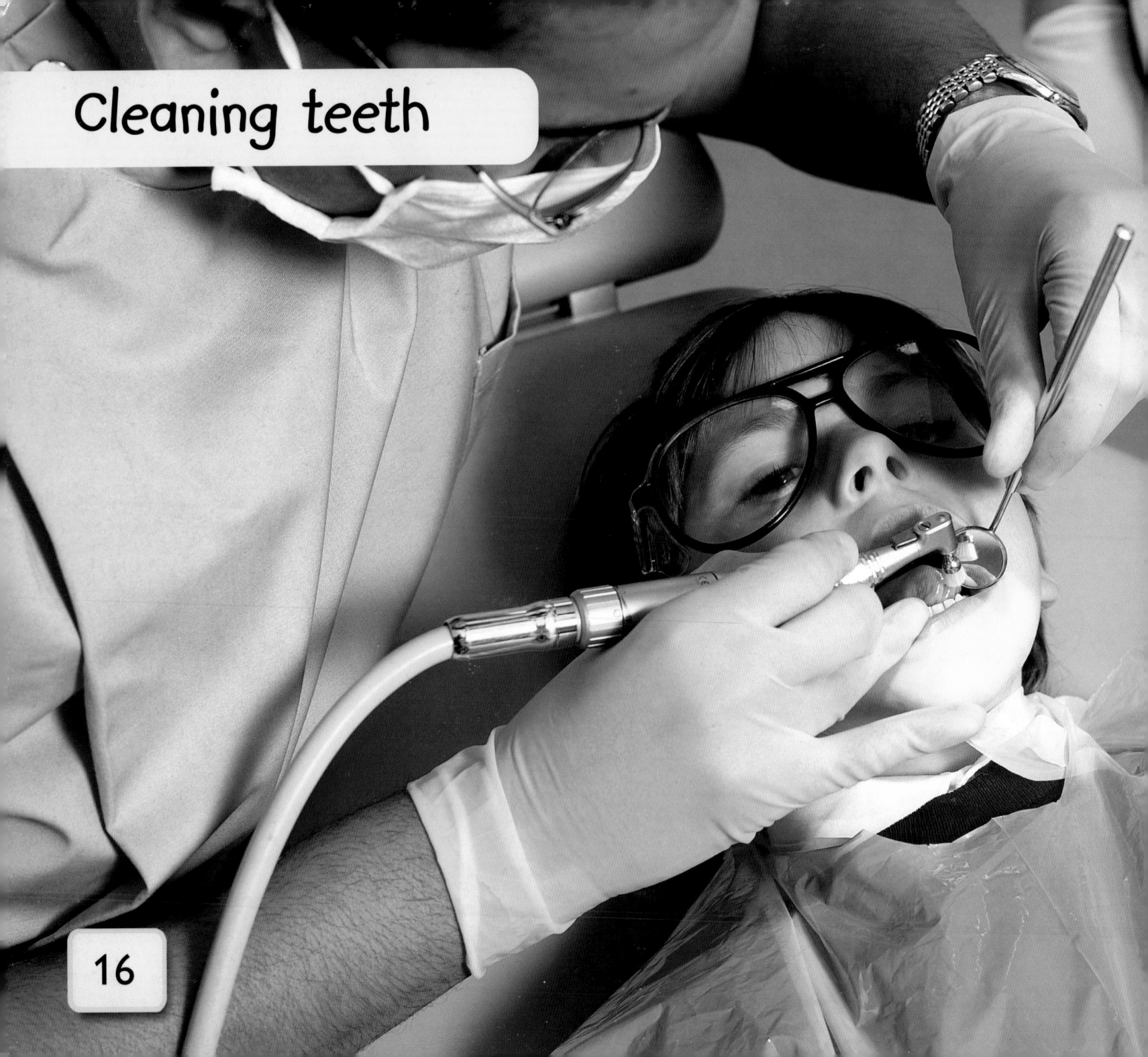

Cleaning teeth

"Now I'm going to clean your teeth," says the dentist.

The toothbrush whirrs round and round.

The toothpaste tastes nice. The toothbrush feels tickly!

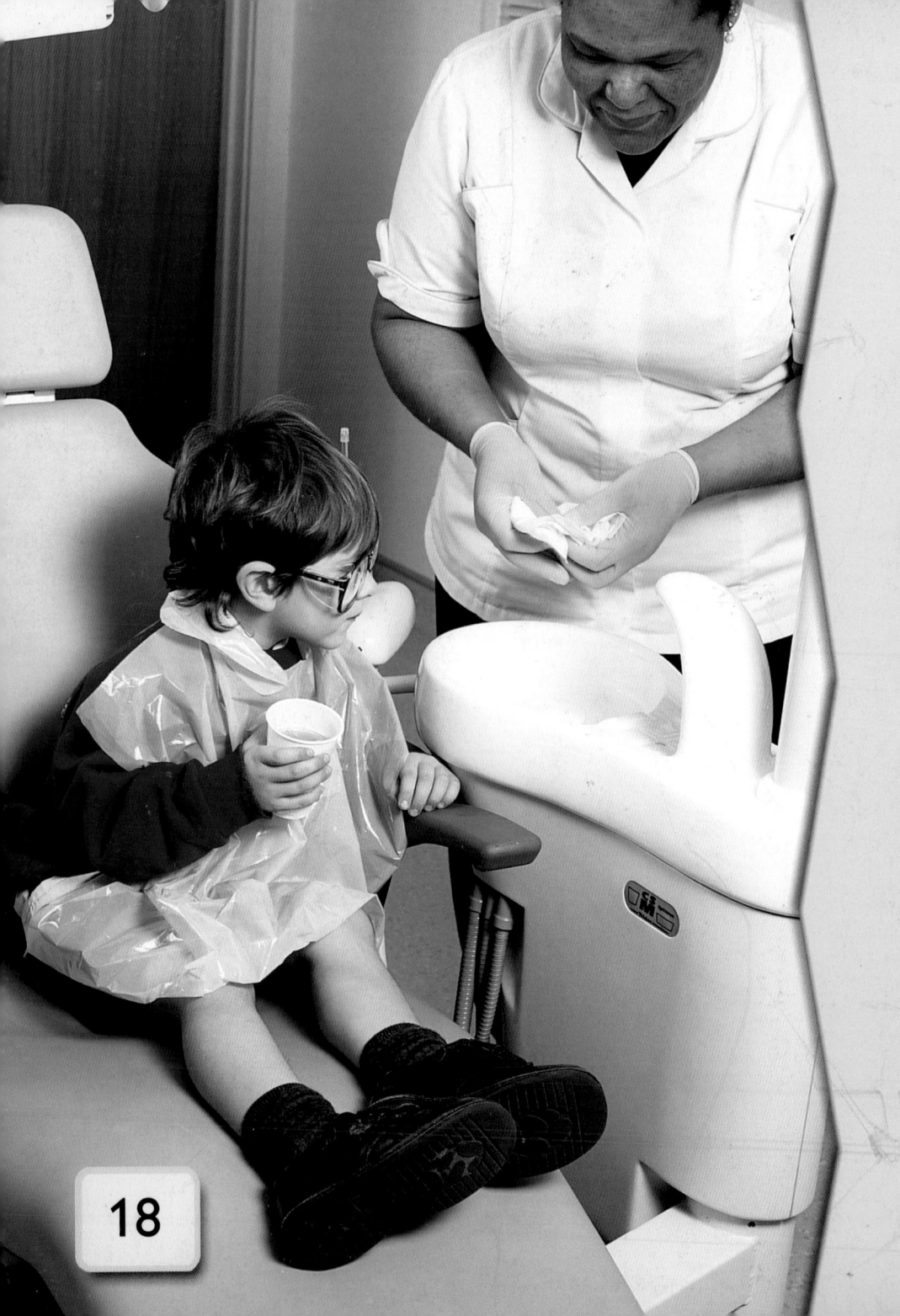

I wash my
mouth with the
pink water.

I spit the water
out into the
little basin.

18

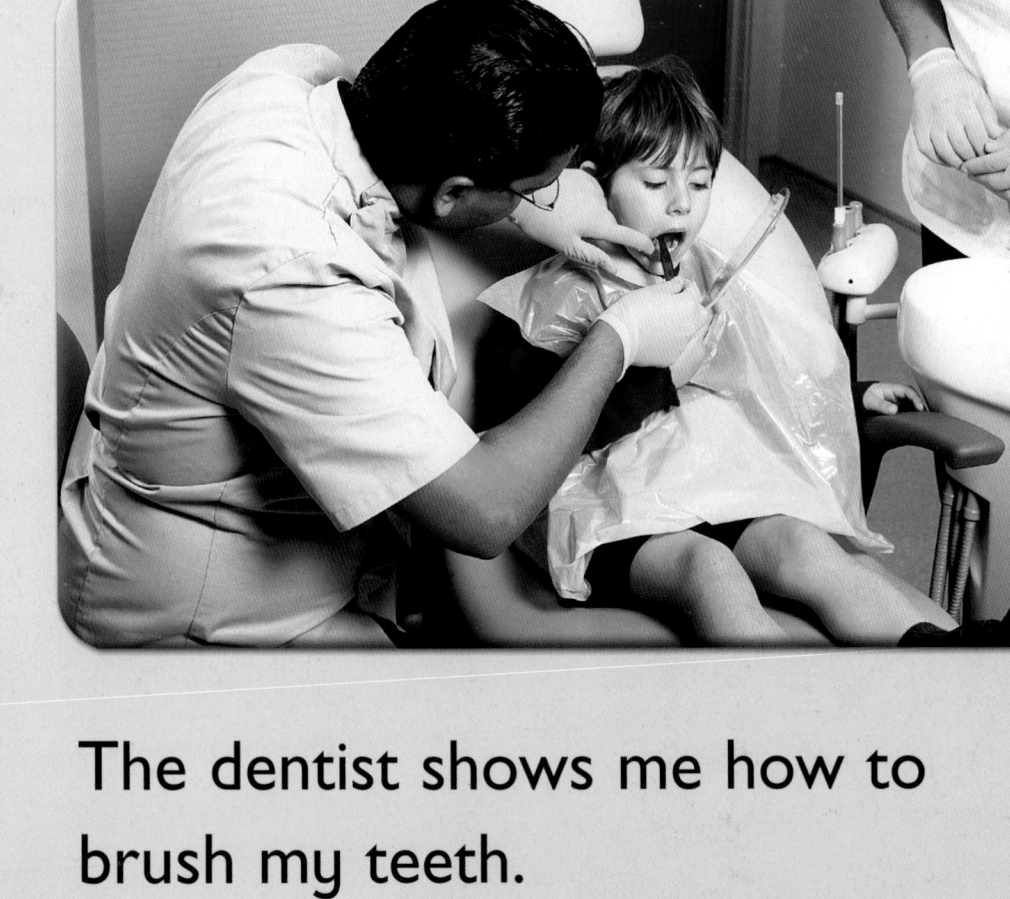

The dentist shows me how to
brush my teeth.

"Brush round and round," he says.

The dentist says, "Well done!"

He gives me a special pack to help me to keep my teeth clean.

I show my brother how to clean his teeth.

"Now you can have a nice smile, too," I say.

Glossary

clean – you clean your teeth to get rid of old bits of food. This keeps your teeth healthy and white.

dentist – a dentist looks after your teeth to keep them strong and healthy.

mouth – you eat and talk with your mouth. Inside your mouth are your teeth and tongue.

teeth – you have twenty teeth inside your mouth. You chew food with your teeth.

Index

Carers' and teachers' notes

- Look at the front cover together. Talk about the picture. Can your child guess what the book is going to be about?
- Point out the title, explaining that it tells us what the book is about. Read the title to your child.
- Has your child been to the dentist? If your child has, talk about his/her visit. What can he/she remember?
- Read the book, discussing the photographs. What is happening in each picture? Explain to your child that the lady on page 10 is a dental nurse, who helps the dentist.
- Identify the contents page, the glossary and the index.
- Look at the contents page together. Point out that it shows the different sections of the book, in the order that they appear. Using the contents, look up the page entitled 'Open wide!'.
- Look at the index. Point out that it is in alphabetical order. Explain that the index tells us where in the book we can find certain information. Use the index to look up the references to 'mouth'.

- Find the words in **bold** type and look them up in the glossary.
- Ask a question about going to the dentist, e.g. 'How do you clean your teeth?' Find the answer using the contents page, the index or the glossary.
- Read the book again, pointing to the words as you say them. Choose an important word, such as 'dentist', to miss out as you read. Encourage your child to say the word every time you miss it out.
- Pick out some key words, e.g. 'dentist', 'teeth', 'clean'. Look at the shape of the words. Make the sound of the letters which start the words. Find these words throughout the book.
- Discuss which foods are good for our teeth and explain why we shouldn't eat too many sugary foods. Talk about how important it is for your child to brush his/her teeth twice a day, in order to keep his/her teeth healthy.
- Role-play a visit to the dentist, taking turns to be the dentist and the patient.